Dear Maryanne,

A Merry Xmas & a great 1992 to you.

lotsa love

Cathy xx

P.S. Always remember what Geraldine Doyle said on Page 41.

'As I Was Saying...'

'As I Was Saying...'

THE WIT & WISDOM *of* AUSTRALIAN WOMEN

Compiled by Margaret Geddes
Cartoons by Judy Horacek

The Five Mile Press
351 Whitehorse Road
Balwyn Victoria 3103

First published 1990
Reprinted 1991

Printed in Singapore by Kyodo Printing Co. Ltd.

National Library of Australia Cataloguing-in-Publication data

'As I Was Saying...'

ISBN 0 86788 267 0.

1. Women - Quotations. 2. Quotations, English - Australia.
I. Geddes, Margaret.

082.082

Contents

So what's your official reason for leaving - I wouldn't have your babies or I wouldn't be your mother?
horacek

Introduction

WHAT a luxury to be asked to compile a book such as this! Few tasks could be more enjoyable.

This is clearly not the definitive collection of Australian women's quotes — you could easily fill another volume, and another. But it is a beginning.

These quotes are drawn from throughout Australia's history, with a bias towards the present. Not all of Australia's founding mothers proved infinitely quotable: Elizabeth Macarthur, for instance, is a font of wisdom — but mainly on the subject of wool.

All the women quoted are Australian or have spent some formative years here (we haven't checked their citizenship papers!). And all have been involved in public life in one way or another, so you will recognise many names. Sadly, many names will be new to you, too, since nothing sinks more quickly in Australia than a wise or witty saying by a woman!

One thing which struck me when I was researching this book was just how far we've come over the years. As Vida Goldstein, a candidate for Kooyong in the Federal election of 1913, said, ' "The world moves slowly, my masters!" Woman's world, especially, but it does move, and that's something to be thankful for.'

We owe so much to these women who went before us. And I owe a great deal to the staffs of the La Trobe Library and the *Age* editorial library, where many of these gems were uncovered, and where I was free to fossick happily for hours.

MARGARET GEDDES
Melbourne, 1990

Are you two alone?
Do you want to tell him or will I?
horacek

Home Truths

*T*HE first rule in opera is the first rule in life: see to everything yourself.

DAME NELLIE MELBA
(1861-1931)

I think it's barbaric when people get married and they lose their privacy. Houses should be built with lots of little rooms so everyone can have a room with a table in it.

ELIZABETH JOLLEY
quoted in the Australian, *1986*

*I*F you write to satisfy your soul, you will satisfy your readers. Not that one ever does succeed in satisfying one's own soul.

MARY GRANT BRUCE
quoted in Billabong's Author, *1979*

I always wanted to be famous, and I didn't much care what I was famous for.

COLLEEN McCULLOUGH
quoted in the Australian, *1989*

❧

THESE days it's a brave woman who can walk the length and breadth of a supermarket with her Iced Vo Vos showing. I hide mine underneath my unprocessed bran.

PAT McDERMOTT

writing in the Australian Women's Weekly, *1988*

❧

I have learned three things in my life: firstly, you can't have everything; secondly, nothing is for nothing — you (or somebody else) has to pay for everything; thirdly, there's a back and a front, a good side and a bad side, to everything.

DAME KATE CAMPBELL

writing in The Half-Open Door, *1982*

❧

SOMETIMES it takes me all day to get a phrase exactly as I see it, to put the salt on the tails of the words I want.

JOAN LINDSAY

quoted in the Age, *Melbourne, 1962*

❧

I learned a great deal about tolerance. When people get fussed, I say to myself, 'Does it really matter?'...I've got a private sense of perspective about matters. When I was a prisoner of the Japanese, the things I missed most were having a comb, a cup of tea and a bit of toast and butter. I still enjoy being able to have talc and soap. I do not take any of these things for granted, even though it is half a lifetime later...

VIVIAN BULLWINKEL

interviewed in Sheilas: A Tribute to Australian Women, *1976*

THERE is only one certainty in life — it will change.

DAME ZARA BATE

quoted in the Sunday Press, *Melbourne, 1978*

YOUR true gentlewoman does not sit down and weep and say, 'I've never done such things' — she simply 'does' and no more about it.

DAISY BATES

quoted in Daisy Bates, *1971*

LOOKING cute's no good...It was much more fun being a wacker! Imagine having to be the magician's helper...that was the dead dreary job, wasn't it?

ROSIE STURGESS

interviewed in It's a Joke, Joyce, *1989*

I believe...that, to appreciate fully the blessings of a happy home, children, friends and books, a trial of lonely bush life for a few years is indispensable.

LOUISA MEREDITH

(1812-1895)

I was a political bride. I married him nineteen years ago and was taken straight to Canberra. It was an awful place in those days — all the men had bald heads. Everything was so ghastly.

TAMIE FRASER

quoted in the Herald, *Melbourne, 1976*

Reflections of an Occasional Cook, Examining the High Shelves in a Kitchen Cupboard.

There should be cloves. There must be cloves, I thought.
I well remember that in 'fifty-nine
I made an apple pie, the classic sort.
The guests (they lied, perhaps?) who came to dine
All voted it successful. Let me see...
Perhaps it's time to turn this cupboard out.
Paprika, garlic salt, and goodness me —
Such a treasure trove! A tin of sauerkraut.
And poppy seeds. Well, yes, I do recall
One brave departure named Veal Madelaine.
Or was it? Anyhow, they ate it all.
The trouble was, the effort seemed in vain.
It tasted very much like flannelette.
And all those poppy seeds! A better cook
Might find a way to use the surplus yet.
What was the reason I began to look?
Those bayleaves I'd forgotten. And some mace.
Such stocks should grace a more accomplished stove.
Perhaps it's time I tidied up the place.
Meanwhile, life's short. What say we skip the clove?

DOROTHY DRAIN

writing in the Australian Women's Weekly, *1962*

WHEN you're young it's very hard to understand that old people feel exactly the same as they felt when they were young. Things get a little less acute, both in misery and in joy, and certainly in expectation. But otherwise, you're essentially the same person.

DAME ROMA MITCHELL,

interviewed in The Matriarchs, *1987*

ALL adulthood really means is defrosting your own chops at night and slaving over your own hot can opener.

KATHY LETTE

Hit and Ms, 1984

AT best the greatest geniuses need other hearts attuned to nurture their lay or it is drought-smitten from the start. 'The listening heart' as I heard an unlettered little Italian girl call it.

MILES FRANKLIN

in a letter to Nettie Palmer, 1929

GOING from having your house cleaned to cleaning others teaches you a bit about how the other half lives.

JOAN CHILD

quoted in the Camberwell Progress Press, *1987*

I experienced real fear for the first time ever at sea...But who wouldn't be happy doing something they love for six uninterrupted months?

KAY COTTEE

1988

MALE and female sexuality exist like 'His' and 'Hers' sweaters. The measurable difference is slight but it is highly significant in its own context.

BEATRICE FAUST

Women, Sex and Pornography, *1980*

❧

WEARING a tiara to a barbecue is not a bad idea. One can impale some snags on it, bow down in front of the hotplate and Bob's your proverbial avuncular figure. However, if you do not wish to draw attention to yourself, it is not advisable. Given that one is likely to be dealing with paper plates, tomato sauce, charcoal, kids and dogs, one is acting sensibly if the Givenchy is left in the wardrobe.

KAZ COOKE

Keep Yourself Nice, the Age, *Melbourne, 1988*

❧

FOR all the churches you can build, and all the books you can export, you will never do much good without what a gentleman in the colony very appropriately called 'God's police' — wives and little children — good and virtuous women.

CAROLINE CHISHOLM

(1808-1877)

❧

WATCH men and women in a social group and the women's contribution will usually begin, 'Oh God, I was so embarrassed the other day when...' The men of course are trying to outdo each other with their 'I can top that' storytelling skills, while the women are vying, in a non-threatening way of course, to see who's been the biggest dill.

WENDY HARMER

It's a Joke, Joyce, *1989*

TIME — whether you are burning it up by falling in love or spreading it out thin in a dentist's waiting room — is a commodity that cannot be weighed out and measured by clocks. The genius who first thought up a concoction of little cogwheels and pulleys and striking bells for the slicing of our days into twenty-four hours has considerably increased the muddle and confusion of the civilised world.

JOAN LINDSAY
Time Without Clocks, *1962*

TAKE a punt, that's what I believe. If you just sit there the days run away. If you make a few boo-boos, who cares? You can shut yourself up in your castle and never come out again, or you can stick in there and keep on trying.

LADY RUPERT CLARKE
quoted in the Age, *Melbourne, 1980*

SOME minds remain open long enough for the truth not only to enter but to pass on through by way of a ready exit without pausing anywhere along the route.

SISTER ELIZABETH KENNY
(1886-1952)

WOMEN were always there, cooking, washing, scrubbing, feeding children and husbands. Without them, there wouldn't be a history, yet history is written as if they weren't there.

KATE GRENVILLE
quoted in the Age, *Melbourne, 1987*

WHEN you write a novel you're not writing about anything really except yourself, which is an awful thought, but how do you know what anyone else thinks? You can't possibly know how they'll react. You can only see a reaction, but your interpretation of it is your own.

THEA ASTLEY

interviewed in Rooms of their Own, *1985*

I know people who can infuse the word 'darling' with unprecedented venom. Others can make 'rat's-breath' into an affectionate nickname. Generally, one is advised to stay away from such people, but you get my drift. Dagginess is in the eye of the beholder, and very often the preferred trouser style of the beholdee.

KAZ COOKE

Keep Yourself Nice, the Age, *Melbourne, 1988*

ART is the expression of 'whatsoever things are lovely', at the same time expressing things unseen — the golden thread running through time.

GRACE COSSINGTON SMITH

quoted in the National Times, *1982*

MISERLINESS is a most secret vice that the miser scrupulously hides from himself and firmly believes no one else can see. Ha! But they can smell it. Miserliness smells like the slightly damp second-hand felt that went under the new carpet ten years ago.

SHARON GRAY

writing in the Age, *Melbourne, 1989*

Remember when Damn was spelt d..n?

Though all my logic tells me
That Women's Lib's the shot
At times I have a niggle —
In some respects it's not.

It used to be amusing
When gentlemen would swear,
Then turn to their companions
And say, "Oh, sorry dear."

We knew, my generation,
These words and plenty more
But liked the implication
They shocked us to the core.

One offers no excuses,
Hypocrisy is done
Forgive me if I mention
We found it rather fun.

DOROTHY DRAIN

writing in the Australian Women's Weekly, *1962*

ONLY by keeping the past alive in our memories can we choose what to discard and what to retain in our present way of life.

LADY CILENTO

My Life, *1987*

I think more of the will to do good and the effort than the actual work done. It may not seem to leave any mark, but I'm sure it does. Nothing is wasted.

DORIS BLACKBURN

in a letter to her fiancé, 1914

❧

I believe that having your cake and eating it too is what it's all about.

SALLYANNE ATKINSON

quoted in Sallyanne, Portrait of a Lord Mayor, *1987*

❧

FORTUNATELY she is free to paint what she pleases and how she thinks. She does not imagine she has advanced in her art — only moved. The ladder of art lies flat, not vertical.

MARGARET PRESTON

from her essay, 'Eggs to Electrolux', Art in Australia, *Margaret Preston issue, 1927*

❧

I must say I try not to read the newspapers at all. I think they cause brain damage...We don't know how bad for us the information is that bombards us every day. I work on the view that if something really significant has happened somebody'll tell you about it.

BLANCHE D'ALPUGET,

interviewed in Rooms of their Own, *1986*

❧

IF I was the oldest in feeling of the young folks in my teens, I am the youngest woman in my eighties, so I have abundant compensation.

CATHERINE HELEN SPENCE

(1825-1910)

Shopping Trolleys

notice how they have perfect steering
until you put something in them

their automatic response is to apply
the brakes, however, they can be goaded forward

by the application of a foot sharply placed
on the bottom bar, surprise is essential.

you can make them move their wheels
but there is no guarantee that they will all

move in the same direction. the poor things
are terrified & want only to escape. an average

family shopping turns them into nervous
wrecks for weeks. you might think that those

trolleys you see out in carparks & under
sapling trees are sight-seeing. they aren't.

they are trying to avoid having things
put in them. it's hopeless. there is always

someone who wants to use them as garbage bins,
laundry baskets, billy carts, flower pots or

bassinettes. they are prolific breeders
in the wild & run enormous herds.

they rust in captivity.

JENNY BOULT
from 'Notes on Suburban Wildlife'

EVERY woman's blessing: 'There but for the grace of God, family, friends and finances, go I,' she says.

THERESE RADIC
writing in Double Time, *1985*

I don't want you to take this the wrong way, but...
Trouble at breakfast time number 103
horacek

For Better or for Worse

I'VE been married but it didn't work for me. I didn't breed well in captivity.

RACHEL BERGER
quoted in the Sydney Morning Herald/Age
Good Weekend, 1989

MOST used husbands come with strings attached and the ghosts of the past are nothing compared to the tangles of the present.

BETTINA ARNDT
All About Us, *1989*

THE first time I fell absolutely, violently, passionately in love...my senses were so heightened that one day we were walking through the park and I swear, I actually heard a leaf drop to the ground.

PAT LOVELL
quoted in the Australian, *1989*

WOMEN think that they marry someone to lean on, but it's men who lean on us.

ROSE SCOTT
(1847-1923)

IF I had married, I don't think I would have been able to paint so much. There was one friend I liked and went to see, but it didn't come to anything because I didn't want to marry. I think it was because I was wholly interested in painting.

GRACE COSSINGTON SMITH
quoted in the National Times, *1982*

I think we had it made being young and single in the late '60's and early '70's. We had freedoms that are unlikely to be there again.

BETTINA ARNDT
quoted in the Sydney Morning Herald/Age *Good Weekend, 1989*

WE need men, even ones who blow their noses in the shower, because they can give us the means to give birth to more feminists, and then we can take over the wor...Sorry, got a bit carried away.

KAZ COOKE
The Modern Girl's Guide to Everything, *1986*

NOT only is my husband most caring, he is also by nature an impossible romantic. He invited me to dinner the moment I gently reminded him it had been our anniversary the previous week.

JANE FRASER
writing in the Australian, *1989*

Eve-Song

I span and Eve span
A thread to bind the heart of man;
But the heart of man was a wandering thing
That came and went with little to bring:
Nothing he minded what we made,
As here he loitered, and there he stayed.

I span and Eve span
A thread to bind the heart of man;
But the more we span the more we found
It wasn't his heart but ours we bound
For children gathered about our knees:
The thread was a chain that stole our ease.
And one of us learned in our children's eyes
That more than man was love and prize.
But deep in the heart of one of us lay
A root of loss and hidden dismay.

He said he was strong. He had no strength
But that which comes of breadth and length.
He said he was fond. But his fondness proved
The flame of an hour when he was moved.
He said he was true. His truth was but
A door that winds could open and shut.

And yet, and yet, as he came back,
Wandering in from the outward track,
We held our arms, and gave him our breast,
As a pillowing place for his head to rest.
I span and Eve span,
A thread to bind the heart of man!

DAME MARY GILMORE
(1865-1962)

EVERY now and then when I'm having one of those little far-away thinkettes to myself that you do sometimes, I just think next time round when I'm reincarnated, I'm coming back as a dumb blonde.

RHONDA SCHEPISI
interviewed in Women on Men, *1987*

COHABITATION means one thing: insomnia. If his hacksaw snores and diagonal sleeping position don't put excess baggage under your eyes, his nocturnal rumblings will. There is definitely something superior about man's digestive tract.

KATHY LETTE
Hit and Ms, *1984*

I was recently suffering from a severe ear infection and forced to make one of my infrequent visits to the doctor. He made me rest for a period but told me that my vocal cords were in such a pristine state that I would sing easily for another fifteen years. I said to him, 'Please don't tell my husband'.

JOAN SUTHERLAND
from Joan Sutherland, *1987*

ONE of the nicest compliments ever paid to me was to be told that I could say the nastiest things of men in the nicest possible way.

ROSE SCOTT
(1847-1925)

NOW, after three months of it [Parliament], I am still excited and oh, thank heaven I'm not in love...I need to be heart-free to work 16 to 18 hours a day.

DAWN FRASER

quoted in the Sun News-Pictorial, *Melbourne, 1988*

A woman finished and fulfilled,
And a completed man...
Each bound to other, yet both free...
It is not, but it ought to be.

ADA CAMBRIDGE

(1844-1926)

I am convinced I fell in love with my husband because he and my father were pretty much the same. I was daddy's little girl and I wanted to stay daddy's little girl forever.

LADY FAIRFAX

quoted in New Idea, *1989*

I like to think that for every drover who sat around a campfire cracking jokes with the boys there was a drover's wife doing the same with the girls in the wattle and daub kitchen.

'The only reason I've had nine children by him is that I was hoping to lose him in the crowd'...pause to crack the snake's back and split redgum stump...'We were married for better or worse, he couldn't have done better and I couldn't have done worse'.

WENDY HARMER

It's a Joke, Joyce, *1989*

❧

*W*HEN we think we are 'in love' is when we are most grossly concerned with plans for our own personal happiness. Having our hearts 'broken' means we didn't get what we want. Love, the desire for the happiness of others, has nothing to do with it.

SHARON GRAY

writing in the Age, *Melbourne, 1989*

❧

from Wife Alone

With you not here
I can play martyr
dully preferring
bread and water

to mangled savouries
sweets and wine
I set for your sake,
you eat for mine.

JUDITH RODRIGUEZ

❧

I was so desperate to keep it [the breakup of her marriage to politician Andrew Peacock] private that after I moved out of the house into a flat, I used to put the garbage out at midnight, with sunglasses on, so no one would recognise me.

MARGARET PEACOCK

quoted in the Sydney Morning Herald/Age *Good Weekend, 1989*

ONE thing we achieved was to make sex less important...Good sex is very unimportant in a marriage. It is getting sex good enough so it can be relegated to the back burner in terms of a marriage. Then it can be what it should be — an extremely good way of achieving some instant intimacy in a relationship where you are up to your knees in kids and hassle.

BETTINA ARNDT
quoted in the Sydney Morning Herald/Age
Good Weekend, 1989

MEN need an awful lot of looking after — by mothers, secretaries, gofers, wives, girlfriends...Perhaps one of the reasons why men don't go to doctors and psychiatrists as often as women is that they don't need to. Women generally do a brilliant job of man-maintenance.

BEATRICE FAUST
interviewed in Women on Men, *1987*

WHEN you go out with a guy you bullshit. You say things like'No, I'm not hungry thankyou — just an entree serve for me,' — 'Oh, no alcohol, just Perrier...' This is absolute crap. When you go out with your girlfriends you don't even bother with knives and forks — you just kneel at the table and tip it in.

RACHEL BERGER
quoted in the Sydney Morning Herald/Age
Good Weekend, 1989

I wouldn't mind my mother's little quirks if I wasn't developing the same ones myself
Uh oh
horacek

The Invisible Cord

CONTRACTION by contraction, the invisible cord pulls us tighter: moon, mother, daughter, baby. Thirty-two years apart, contraction by contraction, I am still linked to my mother. We are again sharing the childbirth bed as I am rocked in the same cradle of pain that saw me into the world: I have inherited the pattern of this labour from her, Fate has handed us the baton of this long, long race and now it is my turn to run with it.

ANNA MARIA DELL'OSO

Cats, Cradles and Chamomile Tea, *1989*

THE best thing I ever did? Why, having a child, my son. What else?

THEA ASTLEY

quoted in the Australian Women's Weekly *1990*

NOTHING brings you back to earth more than coming home from Parliament to two kids for whom the most important issue is whether they can go to the disco that night.

JANINE HAINES

quoted in the Age, *Melbourne, 1986*

ONE would think that more than ten years after Women's Liberation we would be getting our sons' education right. But recently...groups of 13-15 year old girls were asked what they wanted to do when they left school. They all wanted a career... They all wanted to get married. They all wanted to have a family but to continue to work.

The same question was put to boys of the same age... They all said they wanted to have a career... They all wanted to marry and have a family. They would let their wives work...*let* their wives work...until the babies were born. We are still raising cavemen.

ITA BUTTROSE
writing in Cleo, *1982*

BABIES teach their parents an enormous amount. I grew up thinking my parents taught me things, but the reverse is true.

JUDY DAVIS
quoted in the Australian, *1989*

THE plain fact is that they bring you up, rather than the other way around. Oh, for some peace you say, but then they're off on their own, disdaining nice family outings, and you realise, in the silences now descending on the remaining two in the car — the 'old fogeys' — that for years you have relied on 'conversations' dominated by 'sit still'; 'keep your head in'; 'don't argue'; and 'I know you feel sick, but we can't stop here'.

YVONNE PRESTON
writing in the National Times, *1982*

Request to a Year

If the year is meditating a suitable gift,
I should like it to be the attitude
of my great-great-grandmother,
legendary devotee of the arts,

who, having had eight children
and little opportunity for painting pictures,
sat one day on a high rock
beside a river in Switzerland

and from a difficult distance viewed
her second son, balanced on a small ice-floe,
drift down the current towards a waterfall
that struck rock-bottom eighty feet below,

while her second daughter, impeded,
no doubt, by the petticoats of the day,
stretched out a last-hope alpenstock
(which luckily caught him on his way).

Nothing, it was evident, could be done;
and with the artist's isolating eye
my great-great-grandmother hastily sketched the scene.
The sketch survives to prove the story by.

Year, if you have no Mother's Day present planned,
reach back and bring me the firmness of her hand.

Judith Wright

MANY people have said to me 'What a pity you had such a big family to raise. Think of the novels and the short stories and the poems you never had time to write because of that.' And I looked at my children and I said, 'These are my poems. These are my short stories.'

Olga Masters
(1919-1986)

MOTHERHOOD — the mother role — just isn't a very good identity base today. Motherhood is a short-term appointment now. It doesn't last long.

LYN RICHARDS
quoted in the Age, *Melbourne, 1979*

I was going out with a man who said I was mothering him and he was losing his identity and I said, 'Mother you? Mother you? I do not mother you. As for losing your identity, I sew the nametag in the back of your jumper — what more do you want? You'd lose your head if it wasn't screwed on.' He said 'That's it. I'm leaving,' and I said 'Not in those dirty old jeans you're not. You come back here.'

WENDY HARMER
quoted in the Sydney Morning Herald/Age,
Good Weekend, 1989

I think there's a good lesson here. It shows what you can do with age and after a long break, and it also goes to show that a mother's place is not necessarily always at home making beds.

LISA CURRY-KENNY
quoted in the Sunday Age, *Melbourne, 1989*

MEN give life easily and in the main can take it easily but every time a new life is born into the world, a woman suffers...I believe that the taking of life affects women differently to men.

DORIS BLACKBURN
Hansard, 1948

THE white people used to say to Dad: 'That girl walks this land as though she thinks it's hers.' Dad wouldn't say anything. He'd just walk home and tell me, 'Mrs. So-and-so said you walk this land as though you think it's yours'.
'It is mine, isn't it?' I would say. And he'd say 'Yes, girl. Don't ever forget it.'

OODGEROO of the tribe NOONUCCAL,
(formerly KATH WALKER)
interviewed in The Twig is Bent, *1979*

PARENTHOOD is like the modern stonewashing process for denim jeans. You may start out crisp, neat and tough, but you end up pale, limp and wrinkled.

KERRY CUE
Born to Whinge, *1988*

STRANGE that I was given
Thoughts that soar to heaven,
Yet must I sit and keep
Children in their sleep!

DAME MARY GILMORE
(1865-1962)

WOMEN are always rapt in the fact they can produce a child of the opposite sex. When they reproduce a female, they've just reproduced themselves and there's no great joy in that.

COLLEEN McCULLOUGH
quoted in the Australian, *1989*

Cock Crow

Wanting to be myself, alone,
Between the lit house and the town
I took the road, and at the bridge
Turned back and walked the way I'd come.
Three times I took that lonely stretch,

Three times the dark trees closed me round,
The night absolved me of my bonds
Only my footsteps held the ground.

My mother and daughter slept,
One life behind and one before,
And I that stood between denied
Their needs in shutting-to the door.

And walking up and down the road
Knew myself, separate and alone,
Cut off from human cries, from pain,
And love that grows about the bone.

Too brief illusion! Thrice for me
I heard the cock crow on the hill,
And turned the handle of the door
Thinking I knew his meaning well.

ROSEMARY DOBSON

I think actually giving birth to a son is an interesting thing for a woman, particularly if they've got a very strong male aspect, as I have. For me, it was extremely psychologically satisfying, as if there was the male, incarnate. I think that actually did release a creative process.

BLANCHE D'ALPUGET
interviewed in Rooms of their Own, *1985*

A bizarre thing happened to me over the weekend. I was washing the kitchen floor and I heard myself say, 'Gee this Handy Andy brings up these tiles a treat,' and I thought 'Oh my God I'm turning into my mother.' I mean a few years ago the only time I would wash the kitchen floor was if it made a crunch noise when I slept on it. But sooner or later, we all turn into our parents. I don't care who you are, every woman will say at some time in her life, 'Would you mind not walking on that? I've just washed it.' And every man will say, 'Well, the bloody bins don't put themselves out, do they?'

WENDY HARMER

quoted in the Sydney Morning Herald/Age *Good Weekend, 1989*

Mothers and Daughters

Time brushes their faces
taking from one to give to the other

the slow dip and sweep
brushes the hollows down
for the other's

one face wears so thin
even the brush marks are seen
its wither
blooms on the other

one pair of lips
tires
time takes their flesh
in gutters for the other

kiss the thin or the full
there's only one
face

KATE LLEWELLYN

If you could just try to sound less like a woman...
You want me to do animal impersonations?
horacek

Quick Takes

*A*CTING is the most public form of indecent exposure.

RUTH CRACKNELL
quoted in the Australian Women's Weekly, *1987*

*I*T really bores me smoking — I do it to stop my right hand twitching.

THEA ASTLEY
quoted in the Sydney Morning Herald, *1979*

*M*Y mother used to say, 'He who angers you, conquers you!'. But my mother was a saint.

SISTER ELIZABETH KENNY
(1880-1952)

*M*AN is the only animal that strikes his womenfolk.

JEANNIE GUNN
(1870-1961)

❧

YOU have to be suspicious when you line up against girls with moustaches.

MAREE HOLLAND

on steroid use at the Olympic Games, 1988

❧

ONLY a loser finds it impossible to accept a temporary set-back. A winner asks why.

ITA BUTTROSE

quoted in the Age, *Melbourne, 1988*

❧

THE fifties were ten years of foreplay.

GERMAINE GREER

on the Late Clive James Show, *Channel 4, London, 1984*

❧

I loathe being in the public eye. But it's like washing up, it's something you've just got to do.

TAMIE FRASER

quoted in the Age, *Melbourne, 1975*

❧

GIVE a book a Miles Franklin Award and it sinks without trace.

THEA ASTLEY

quoted in the Sydney Morning Herald, *1979*

❧

LAND rights for gay whales.

MARGRET ROADKNIGHT

coined this 'ultimate cause' slogan at a Bob Hudson concert in Adelaide, 1979

WHAT does 'old' mean, anyway? Does it mean you stay home a lot?

EILEEN BOND

quoted in the Sydney Morning Herald/Age, *Good Weekend, 1990*

FOR me there is always the rainbow beyond the hill.

DAISY BATES

quoted in Daisy Bates, *1971*

A radical celibate is a person with a sense of humour.

ITA BUTTROSE

the Australian, *1987*

IF I'd been a housemaid I'd have been the best in Australia — I couldn't help it. It's got to be perfection for me.

DAME NELLIE MELBA

(1861-1931)

FUNNY women are everywhere you look...we were just waiting for a break in the conversation.

WENDY HARMER

It's a Joke, Joyce, *1989*

❧

WHEN you're on top of the world you should remember it turns over every 24 hours.

TAMIE FRASER

quoted in the Herald, *Melbourne, 1976*

❧

I think churches are a human institution mostly dedicated to getting rich.

COLLEEN McCULLOUGH

quoted in the Australian, *1989*

❧

LIFE is too short to waste on the admiration of one man.

ROSE SCOTT

(1847-1923)

❧

THE pessimists, like the poor, we have always with us.

DAISY BATES

quoted in Daisy Bates, *1971*

❧

SOMEONE once told me that acting is a child's game with adult rules.

NICOLE KIDMAN

quoted in the Australian Women's Weekly, *1989*

❧

TO be born is to be lucky.

KYLIE TENNANT

Ride On Stranger, *1943*

BOOBS are back in the 1990s. I'm just so glad I didn't throw out my old ones.

MANDY SOLOMON

speaking at the International Women's Day lunch, Melbourne, 1990

READING it *[The Thorn Birds]* is rather like struggling through a year's issues of the *Women's Weekly* in one sitting.

DOROTHY GREEN

The Music of Love, *1984*

MY mother told me that men are like seagulls — you should never look up to them.

GERALDINE DOYLE

on Couchman, ABC TV, 1989

BEHIND every man there's a victim of circumstances.

JANINE HAINES

writing in the Australian Women's Weekly, *1987*

I don't care what you say, for me or against me, but for heaven's sake say *something* about me.

DAME NELLIE MELBA

(1865-1931)

I'm off to my hobby now dear -see you this evening
horacek

Fight the Good Fight

WE have survived 40,000 years. They tried to rape us, they tried to murder us, they tried to burn us out. They took our land, they took our kids, they tried to breed us out — the whole bang lot. We survived all that and we are still going to be here when they are gone. That's how I figure it. So we just have to hang in here.

PAT O'SHANE

quoted in the Age, *Melbourne,1985*

ALL that baiting about why there are no women artists or composers, no women generals or women on the boards of companies, when the question should have been why there are no great women rapists, mass murderers, cut-throats and war-mongerers, no great male nurses, home-makers, child rearers? Oh, what a load of rubbish and conniving it's all been.

ANNA MARIA DELL'OSO

Cats, Cradles and Chamomile Tea, *1989*

IF you want real practical wisdom, go to an old washer-woman patching clothes on the Rocks, with a black eye, and you'll hear more true philosophy than a Parliament of men will talk in a twelvemonth.

LOUISA LAWSON

writing in the Bulletin, *1896*

My Love

Possess me? No, I cannot give
The love that others know,
For I am wedded to a cause:
The rest I must forgo.

You claim me as your very own,
My body, soul and mind;
My love is my own people first,
And after that, mankind.

The social part, the personal
I have renounced of old;
Mine is a dedicated life,
No man's to have and hold.

Old white intolerance hems me round,
Insult and scorn assail;
I must be free, I must be strong
To fight and not to fail.

For there are ancient wrongs to right,
Man's malice to endure;
A long road and a lonely road,
But oh, the goal is sure.

OODGEROO of the tribe NOONUCCAL (formerly KATH WALKER)

THE role of the 'mother figure' for a politician, however, has its drawbacks...Whatever I said in Parliament about the family and kindred subjects was snapped up and recorded; I was the Parliamentary expert in that field! But often statements of far more weight and importance on other matters were unrecorded...In fact, my references to the family were generally incidental to the development of other themes.

DAME ENID LYONS

Among the Carrion Crows, *1972*

❧

LIKE many women in the public eye, I'm damned if I do and damned if I don't. If I raise questions of pornography, child abuse, incest, domestic violence, they say I am obsessed with sex. If I raise equality of opportunity, difficulties women face, they say I'm a man-hating feminist. If I'm flippant about myself it's lacking of confidence; if I'm flippant about them, I'm a sarcastic bitch. If I make strong statements I'm aggressive; if I'm not, I'm weak. If I'm angry, I'm 'emotional'.

JANINE HAINES

quoted in the Age, *Melbourne, 1986*

❧

THE day we've got there will be the day nobody is saying how wonderful it is that we've got a woman in the High Court. They will just accept that there was a woman who had the capacity to do it.

JOAN CHILD

quoted in the Camberwell Progress Press, *1987*

❧

I don't think you get any real social improvement unless people fight for it. It's always been my view that when people have privileges...they'll hang on to them like grim death.

SUSAN RYAN

quoted in the Age, *Melbourne, 1983*

❧

EQUALITY is a meaningless abstraction unless it is founded on economic security and economic strength.

MARY GAUDRON,

quoted in the National Times, *1985*

❧

*I*F the women's movement can be summed up in a single phrase, it is 'the right to choose'.

BEATRICE FAUST

interviewed in Tall Poppies, *1984*

❧

I don't like being put in boxes. If people put you in a box, your ability to help others is restricted. That was the greatest problem with the black movement, keeping it from being possessed by political groups. Academics tried to take us over, neurotic surburban housewives tried to take us over to decorate their green lawns like little black gnomes, the Liberal Party tried to take us over, the Labor Party tried to take us over.

FAITH BANDLER

interviewed in Sheilas: A Tribute to Australian Women, *1976*

❧

I believed that people would come to my meetings out of curiosity, to see the wild woman who sought to enter Parliament. They came, they saw, I conquered; that is, my arguments did.

VIDA GOLDSTEIN

(1869-1949)

❧

*N*O country can advance unless its women advance.

MAIE CASEY

(1891-1983)

EARLY on in life, I learnt that it was wise to try to understand the people who run the joint. It's one of women's survival mechanisms, isn't it? How to second guess, out-wit, outsmart, run rings around and manipulate, men.

ROBYN DAVIDSON
writing in the Age, *Melbourne, 1985*

I have followed the Women's Movement with considerable interest and I always thought it had to be supported. Whenever people moaned about it to me, I'd say 'look at the suffragettes. If they hadn't carried on the way they did, women wouldn't have had the Vote.'

DAME ROMA MITCHELL
interviewed in The Matriarchs, *1987*

THE position of women has undoubtedly improved through their ability to earn money. There's no doubt that people's status is judged by the amount of money they've got, and when women were dependent on their husbands for everything, they had no power. The inferiority of women was due to the three 'Ms': muscle, maternity and money.

DAME KATE CAMPBELL
writing in The Half-Open Door, *1982*

THE basic problem is not that women use cosmetics, that's perfectly all right, but that they have been sold out to believe they are not attractive if they don't.

ELIZABETH REID
quoted in New Idea, *1973*

*A*T first the men would say 'How can you stand the strain of the long debates at night?' but I pointed out that looking after sick babies, and even a sick husband, at night was a good apprenticeship for keeping wide awake. I often see the men around me asleep, while I am following what is going on.

EDITH COWAN

interviewed in Woman's World, *1922*

*O*NE time we did it [marched into Parliament and demanded to see an MP], the attendant said, 'You'll have to wait ten minutes,' and a black woman with us, who was quietly knitting, said, 'Oh, that's all right. We've been waiting for 200 years.' Very softly, she said it. The black women have been the backbone of the whole thing.

FAITH BANDLER,

interviewed in Sheilas: A Tribute to Australian Women, *1976*

*W*OMEN are what men make them. Why, a woman can't bear a child without it being received into the hands of a male doctor; it is baptized by a fat old male; a girl goes through life obeying laws made by men; and if she breaks them, a male magistrate sends her to gaol where a male warden handles her and looks in her cell at night to see if she's alright. If she gets so far as to be hanged, a male hangman puts the rope around her neck; she is buried by a male gravedigger; and she goes to a heaven ruled over by a male God or a hell managed by a male devil. Isn't it a wonder men didn't make the devil a woman?

LOUISA LAWSON

(1848-1920)

As soon as feminist became a term to label certain women, people would say to me 'Look at what you've done. And you're not a feminist'. And I would say 'I am a feminist'. I think the feminists probably thought I was a bit old hat in the beginning, but I refused not to be associated with them.

DAME ROMA MITCHELL
interviewed in The Matriarchs, *1987*

IT'S time to throw aside artificial modesty, all of you. I tell you, woman, that it is a woman's duty to try to save, help and raise woman.

HENRIETTA DUGDALE
(1826-1918)

As to attempting to repeal the laws of nature we should be so obliged if the writer would forward to our office an authenticated copy of the said laws. We presume he must have a copy by him to refer to, but we want the original edition and not his revised version. The 'New Woman' has searched far and wide for an authoritative exposition of the laws of nature, as she has always felt a certain difficulty about attempting to repeal a law until she knew what that law was.

'GODIVA'
in a column in the Champion, *1895*

LIKE it or not, true liberation for women will be achieved only with the full co-operation of men.

ITA BUTTROSE
writing in Cleo, *1982*

I think it is a marvellous movement, and it's a movement that has occurred again and again over the centuries, and at last I think it has a chance of succeeding. Biology has defeated it before, always, but with contraception as it is today, it has a chance. Mind you, as all of us know, there are gains and losses, but there have been great gains.

JESSICA ANDERSON

interviewed in Rooms of their Own, *1986*

NO one would ever say that a male actor was brave because he allowed himself to look plain.

ROBYN NEVIN

interviewed in Tall Poppies, *1984*

THE sooner women learn to respect each other's individual differences the more chance the women's movement has of getting lasting change.

BEATRICE FAUST

interviewed in Tall Poppies, *1984*

WHY join a women's group to lobby government ministers when you can become a minister yourself?

PAULINE TONER

quoted in the Australian Women's Weekly, *1982*

IF I were Pope I would immediately cut off all funding for tertiary institutions and funnel it into the care and nurturing of pregnant women and children under five. Pump all the money at the beginning because once you get to high school it's too late, the kids are wrecked!

BEATRICE FAUST
interviewed in Tall Poppies, *1984*

'THE world moves slowly, my masters!' Woman's world, especially; but it does move, and that's something to be thankful for.

VIDA GOLDSTEIN
(1869-1949)

THE black community has got so little, to be shared by so many. Anybody who goes out there and gets hold of a little bit more and brings it back and shares it around — you think we're going to be ashamed of that? That's survival...

MUM SHIRL (Colleen Shirley Perry)
quoted in Mum Shirl, *1981*

COLLECT in the streets for Belgium and eight thousand, eight hundred pounds is the result; collect for unemployed women — ten pounds sixteen.

VIDA GOLDSTEIN
(1869-1949)

I would like to assure those privileged males that the vibrations coming from the women's section of the Liberal Party at the moment are not being produced by the stirring of teaspoons. They are the boiling resentments of rejected recommendations, and political exclusion at a time when the future of women in Australian society is stalled at the crossroads of indecision.

DAME BERYL BEAUREPAIRE
writing in the Herald, *Melbourne, 1973*

*A*BOVE all, you find you have joined a huge sisterhood. What stands out from those years are the women who came from everywhere. We all found it hard to believe that there were so many other women who have been just as bewildered and unhappy in the role society had allotted them, and sharing the same huge guilt because they did not enjoy the role.

JOYCE NICHOLSON
writing in Double Time, *1985*

I spend a lot of my time talking to women and to women's groups trying to convince them that the experiences they've had in life are as valid as any experiences men have had. I think that needs to be said again and again.

CAROLINE HOGG
interviewed in Women on Men, *1987*

DO not forget that in this wicked world, people take you at your own valuation, so make a big noise. That is what men do!

JESSIE STREET
quoted in Jessie Street, *1978*

THERE are bound to be questions of tokenism — token women, token Queenslanders, token Tasmanians, but if you like to turn the argument around, there have been a lot of token bloody men out there for a long time.

SENATOR MARGARET REYNOLDS
quoted in the Australian, *1988*

BUT I've worked more than twenty years to establish my own name. Why shouldn't I have it? After all, Richardson was the name I was born with — and perhaps I place an almost oriental valuation on a personal name; anyway, why should a woman lose her name on marriage? As for Henry, well, Maurice Guest appeared at a time of feminist agitation, and I wanted the book to be a test. No one, positively no reviewer, spotted it as 'just a woman's work'. Handel — an uncle in Ireland — rather musical, adapted it, and I took it over. My husband rejoiced that I wasn't merely Mrs J.G. Robinson.

HENRY HANDEL RICHARDSON
(1870-1946)

'Sunburnt country' used to be a nice poetic image
Yeah - before there was a hole in the ozone layer
Menu
horacek

I Love a Sunburnt Country...

HERE you've got to be dragged along the ground; you've got to pay your dues. I've grown up with that. And somehow, I don't feel I'm allowed to be rich or have a posh car. My dad's always saying: 'You've earned it! Go and spend some money, do something for yourself'. It takes a while for me to think that, yeah, maybe I should.

KYLIE MINOGUE

quoted in the Australian, *1989*

AUSTRALIANS loathe success that doesn't take place in a scrum. And in Australia you've got to come first — it's not a matter of playing well. It's an attitude that carries through from sport to every other strand of life.

THEA ASTLEY

quoted in the Sydney Morning Herald, *1979*

THE other day I was interviewed on television on that old chestnut of why Australians go away. Actually, I thought it was why, having gone away, Australians should bother to come back.

CHARMIAN CLIFT

The World of Charmian Clift, *1970*

It is incredible, and very embarrassing for many of us, that it has taken 200 years for invading Europeans to have the grace to say to Aboriginal people: 'You were here first'.

Senator Jo Vallentine
quoted in the Age, *Melbourne, 1988*

A really wholehearted devotion to public affairs is considered much less womanly than having three or four kinds of cake for supper and highly polished floors.

Myra Roper
quoted in the Sydney Morning Herald, *1960*

If we love Australia and the Australian people, we must realise, surely, that Australia will only have a culture with any roots in reality, and worthy of the infinite beauty and wealth of her natural resources, when the foundations of our natural life are based on the right of her people to satisfaction of the everyday needs of existence.

Katharine Susannah Prichard
in her essay 'Australia' *1936*

Like most people I think of how we could have handled it [the dismissal of the Labor Government] differently. I mean, I am always saying to Gough: 'Why didn't you just tear it up and say it is your word against mine?'

Margaret Whitlam
quoted in the Sun News-Pictorial, *Melbourne, 1977*

WHEN will some new Australian poet rise
To all the height and glory of his theme?
Nor on the sombre side forever dream —
Our bare, baked plains, our pitiless blue skies,
'Neath which the haggard bushman strains his eyes
To find some waterhole or hidden stream
To save himself and flocks in want extreme!
This is not all Australia! Let us prize
Our grand inheritance! Had sunny Greece
More light, more glow, more freedom, or more mirth?
Ours are wide vistas bathed in purest air —
Youth's outdoor pleasures, Age's indoor peace —
Where could we find a fairer home on earth
Which we ourselves are free to make more fair?

CATHERINE HELEN SPENCE
(1825-1910)

I believe that if non-Aboriginal Australians allow themselves to share Aboriginal culture, history, allow themselves to feel part of this land, then we will develop a collective memory, a deep sense of belonging.

PAT O'SHANE
writing in the Age, *Melbourne, 1986*

I remember that my father used to say that the air of our home town was worth a quid a whiff. I hope he was as much of a crank as I thought then. It would be awful if he was prophetic.

CHARMIAN CLIFT
The World of Charmian Clift, *1970*

AUSTRALIAN women are dogged with domesticity.

MAIE CASEY
(1891-1983)
quoted in the Bulletin, *1952*

TOO many Australians still subscribe to the view: 'If it moves, shoot it. If it doesn't, chop it down or dig it up.'

SENATOR JO VALLENTINE
writing in the Age, *Melbourne, 1988*

SOMETIMES one feels in Australia that nothing fails like success.

DAME LEONIE KRAMER
in an address to the Journalists' Club, Sydney, 1983

HERE I am in my 45th year of exile!

GEORGIANA McCRAE
(1804-1890), quoted in Double Time, *1985*

[ON the occasion of the US Vice-President Dan Quayle's visit to Australia] They walk all over us, they ignore us, and then they send their bloody vice-president, who is about as useful as a hip pocket on a singlet, to make us feel good.

JANINE HAINES
quoted in the Australian *1989*

AS far as I can see, the only difference in this country between a tax collector and a taxidermist is that the taxidermist leaves the skin.

CHRISTINA HINDHAUGH

I Love A Sunburnt Torso, *1987*

IF washing a man's dirty clothes is good enough for a woman to do, why shouldn't a man wash his wife's clothes? There's a peculiar belief in Australia that a woman was born to be a drudge — and she believes it too.

EVE MAHLAB

writing in the Australian, *1978*

I should like to die quietly and fertilize this beautiful soil of Australia, which is far better than anything we try to say about it.

KATHARINE SUSANNAH PRICHARD

in a letter to George Robertson in 1930

OUR land is a beautiful land, a spiritual place, a place to be cared for. But the British, having lost the American War of Independence, saw it as only fit for the dumping of what they called the human scum of the hulks of the River Thames. Australia, a suitable place for a human garbage dump.

EVE MUNGWA FESL

writing in the Age, *Melbourne, 1988*

❧

*I*N my family everything positive has come from the black side, everything negative from the white. You can see why I identified black.

SALLY MORGAN
quoted in the Sydney Morning Herald/Age
Good Weekend 1989

❧

from A Sunburnt Country

I love a sunburnt country
A land of sweeping plains,
Of ragged mountain ranges,
Of droughts and flooding rains.
I love her far horizons.
I love her jewel-sea,
Her beauty and her terror —
The wide brown land for me!

DOROTHEA MACKELLAR
(1885-1968)

❧

Acknowledgements

The Publishers have made every effort to trace the poets whose works are quoted in this volume, and apologise for any omissions which may have unwittingly occurred. They express their gratitude to the following poets and publishers:

Australian Consolidated Press and the Australian Women's Weekly for 'Reflections of an Occasional Cook' and ' Remember When Damn was Spelt D..m?' by Dorothy Drain.

Collins/Angus & Robertson Publishers for 'Cock Crow' by Rosemary Dobson from *Selected Poems,* 1980; 'Eve-song' by Mary Gilmore from *Selected Verse,* 1948, and an untitled poem by Mary Gilmore; and 'Request to a Year' by Judith Wright from *Collected Poems,* 1971.

Curtis Brown (Aust.) for a stanza from 'My Country' by Dorothea Mackellar.

Jacaranda Wiley for 'My Love' by Oodgeroo of the tribe Noonuccal (formerly Kath Walker) from *My People.*

University of Queensland Press for two stanzas of 'Wife Alone' by Judith Rodriguez from *The House by Water.*

Acknowledgement is also gratefully made to the National Gallery of Victoria and Mrs. M.F. Neylon for permission to reproduce *Girl in a Hammock* by Ruth Sutherland; and to Judy Horacek for permission to reproduce the cartoons in this volume.

Cover fabric reproduced by permission of Wilson's Fabrics & Wallcoverings Pty. Ltd.

Further Reading

Publishing details of books from which we have reproduced short extracts (other than those written by the person being quoted) are given below:

BARKER, A.W. *Dear Robertson.* Angus & Robertson, Sydney, 1982.

BROWNFOOT, JANICE & SCOTT, DIANNE *The Unequal Half — Women in Australia since 1788.* Reed Education, Sydney, 1977.

ELLISON, JENNIFER *Rooms of their Own* Penguin Books Australia, Melbourne, 1986.

FABIAN, SUSAN & LOH, MORAG *The Changemakers.* Jacaranda Wiley, Queensland, 1983.

GRIMSHAW, PATRICIA & STRAHAN, LYNNE *The Half-Open Door.* Hale & Tremonger, Sydney, 1982.

HILTON, MARGOT *Women on Men.* McPhee Gribble/Penguin Books Australia, Melbourne, 1987.

LAKE, MARILYN & KELLY, FARLEY *Double Time — Women in Victoria: 150 Years.* Penguin Books Australia, Melbourne, 1985.
LANE, TERRY *The Twig is Bent.* Dove, Melbourne, 1979.
LARKINS, JOHN *Sheilas: A Tribute to Australian Women.* Rigby, Adelaide, 1976.
MATTHEWS, BRIAN *Louisa.* McPhee Gribble/Penguin Books Australia, Melbourne, 1987.
MITCHELL, SUSAN *The Matriarchs.* Penguin Books Australia, Melbourne, 1987.
MITCHELL, SUSAN *Tall Poppies.* Penguin Books Australia, Melbourne, 1984.
MURRAY-SMITH, STEPHEN *The Australian Dictionary of Quotations.* Heinemann, Melbourne, 1984.
PALMER, NETTIE *Fourteen Years: 1925-1939,* Meanjin Press, Melbourne, 1948.
SALTER, ELIZABETH, *Daisy Bates.* Angus & Robertson, Sydney, 1971.
SEKULESS, PETER *Jessie Street.* UQP, Brisbane, 1978.
SYKES, BOBBY *Mum Shirl.* Heinemann, Melbourne, 1981.

Who Said What